CONTENTS

PREFACE: LEARN IT, BE IT, LEAD IT

1. MUNCIE

2. HEAVEN & HELL

3. LEARNING THE SYSTEM

4. THE THRILL OF IT ALL

5. BAD CHECKS

6. BEHIND BARS

7. BEARS OF VEGAS

8. MIKE

9. 2021

EPILOGUE

PREFACE:

LEARN IT,

BE IT, LEAD IT

Learn it, be it, lead it. These six simple words can be seen plastered across billboards along the highway of my life, from Muncie to Florida, Kentucky to Las Vegas and everywhere in between and beyond.

I've been in plenty of situations along the road where I've learned what not to do, what to do, how to do it, and what not to say to avoid getting into more trouble. So I've been there, done that, experienced it. Now it's my turn to lead it and that's how this book came to be.

As of this writing, I'm 45 years old. One thing I've learned is that I forget things if I don't get them down on paper. Yet what you're about to read brought back memories, both good and bad, people I've long forgotten, and secrets that I've kept hidden and buried so deep they might surprise you. On occasion, they've even surprised my husband, Mike. "You've never told me that!" He'll exclaim, and we've been together sixteen years!

As with any life lesson, you have to learn the hard lessons for yourself before you can be an example to others. You have to soak up new experiences like a sponge, and if you can't learn from them then obviously all you're doing is talking a bunch of bullshit.

Once you've absorbed those life lessons, next you've got to be the lesson. You have to lead by example and show people the integrity that comes with experience. Something else I've always told myself is, "I'm never going to ask you to do something I'm not going to do." What do I mean by that? If I'm not going to scrub a toilet, I sure as hell am not going to ask you to scrub a toilet. I'm not going to ask you to paint a wall or get underneath a sink to fix something if I'm not willing to do so myself. That kind of leadership is something I've always practiced in my dealings with other people. I'm not going to ask you to do anything unless I'm willing to do it myself.

Once you've accomplished the first two-learning the hard lessons then embodying the lessons you've learned- you get to teach them to others. If you haven't learned your lesson, you're not going to be able to teach it, because all you're going to do is screw up someone else's life. That's definitely not what I'm trying to do here. Instead, I'm telling this story so that you might learn from my mistakes and successes, too. The rest is ultimately up to you. If I can help someone else out, then that's just another reason why this book came into being.

I had a rough childhood but was always given whatever I wanted by my parents, who also taught me the value of a strong work ethic. I was going to need it, if I was to prove that I was better and stronger than all the kids at school, some of whom teased me unmercifully. As a teenager I found Christ, and at the same time discovered my sexuality. I was the youngest McDonald's manager in the whole of the McOpCo Corporation at one point.

I left home at seventeen, married at eighteen, and was divorced and in jail by the time I was nineteen. If I could go back and do my life over, I would never have gotten married. I would never have hidden who I was. I served over two years in an Indiana prison for writing bad checks, of which I wrote many and with which I bought the most outlandish things. When I came out to my parents, I was in jail. I wrote a letter to them because they needed to hear about who I really was directly from me.

In the years following my release from prison, I looked for love in bars and steamy bathhouses until I found my heart's desire, Mike, in the most unlikely of places-Las Vegas, where I owned and operated a chain of cell phone stores. In 2002, I entered the real estate business and then moved to property management, and now Mike and I own eight homes and live comfortably. Life can be sweet, but not until we taste the sour parts first.

Perhaps in telling my story, I can shine some perspective on other kids' lives before they go through the same crap I put myself through. Who knows? Maybe my story will help out one of a billion struggling, young gay men. It means a lot to me just to be able to tell the story that I've hidden for so long. It can't hurt my career at this point, so why

LEARN IT, BE IT, LEAD IT

not do it now? To have the courage to tell my story is an achievement in itself.

I'm 45 years old and retired. I haven't reached the pinnacle of my life, nor learned every lesson there is to be learned, but I'm eager to continue this journey, and like every journey, it must begin somewhere.

Mine begins in Muncie...

MUNCIE

> was born on a Tuesday, August 17th, 1976 in Muncie, Indiana, the eldest son of Ken and Mary Byrd.

> A once-thriving blue-collar factory worker community, Muncie is basically a one-horse town with about six stoplights that the Ball Brothers, Muncie's claim to fame, built from nothing. They not only founded Ball State University but also the Ball Bros. Glass Manufacturing Company, which operated a Ball mason jar factory in Muncie up until a few years ago. I was even born at Ball Memorial Hospital, now Indiana University Health, as was everyone else, since it was the only major hospital in Muncie.

If you ever drove or were driven in a GM vehicle or flew in a jet plane in the not-too-distant past, a piece of Muncie likely got you to where you were going. My father worked at and retired from Ontario Forge. Later, it became Aeroforge in the early 1990s, when the North American Free Trade Agreement came about. If you flew in a jet engine in the 1980s to the early '90s, my father would've helped

LEARN IT, BE IT, LEAD IT

forge the propeller that went inside the jet engine. My dad would always bring home stories about making giant propellers for these jets. Muncie was not immune to the economic downturns the rest of the country experienced, and eventually, the factories closed down. Most of them are now parking lots.

To visit Muncie these days is to avoid potholes and see strip malls, once glorious and bustling shopping centers, now home to flea markets and fast-food restaurants. In fact, Muncie is home to an inordinate number of fast-food restaurants, one of which, McDonald's, prominently figures into my story a little later.

Many of Muncie's residents can claim kin or family in Tennessee. Without getting too deep into history, at some point in the past, Muncie is where many Tennesseans ended up. I remember one time in Social Studies class, the teacher asked us if anyone had family in Jamestown, Kentucky, and almost every hand in the room, including mine, went up.

My father's side of the family is from Jamestown, but my father was born and raised in Muncie. He served in Vietnam from 1965 to '66 in an area of South Vietnam along the Dong Nai River in what's known as War Zone D. During his tour of duty, he was struck by a piece of mortar shrapnel in his leg after stepping on a landmine and was awarded the Purple Heart for his valor and service. He hasn't ever spoken to me about the particulars of this period of time, but the effects of his service became apparent in other ways.

LEARN IT,
BE IT,
LEAD IT

The house we grew up in on Dayton Street in Muncie had a huge living room that sprawled across the entire length of the house, from one corner to the other. We lived there for about eighteen years before my folks sold it and bought their dream home. The front door led into the kitchen, and all-around could be seen my mother's striking choice of wallpaper, in oranges, yellows, and greens. Covering the walls were wicker and chicken-themed decorations-my mother's sense of interior design in the '70s. We had either shit brown or lime green appliances, and I remember my dad and uncle struggling to install our first dishwasher.

We had three bedrooms. I shared my bedroom with my brother, Scottie, while my brother Jerred got the smallest bedroom. My parents' room had green carpeting with a scallop design, the same pattern as the carpeting in the living room, which had carpeted baseboards. The carpet came up about four inches off the floor.

I remember Euchre nights when I was a kid. The whole family would get together, and there'd be plenty of food and drinks. My aunt would make this big bowl of chips and dip, and they would all play Euchre or Uno for hours. My brothers and I would go to bed and they would still be up playing cards!

Don't get the impression that my childhood was *The Brady Bunch,* because it wasn't. My dad was a very angry, alcoholic man. I remember waking up in the middle of the night because of my dad's screams. At his worst, I remember

LEARN IT, BE IT, LEAD IT

some occasions where mom would have to pull dad off of me when he was beating the shit out of me, usually after he came home from the second shift at the forge after eleven o'clock in the evening. Whatever I did, mom would get at me first, then dad second, who would drag me out of the bunk bed and let me have it.

My mother and her family hailed from Versailles, Kentucky. To this day, she is one of the sweetest people on the planet. Through it all, she's been my best friend since the beginning, and when my dad's temper got the better of him, my mother always stood up to him in my defense. For that, I can never express how grateful I am for her love and protection in those moments.

For example, one of my earliest memories I actually recalled during a therapy session. Before I went to prison, my attorney, hoping to soften the judge's sentence, sent me to a therapist. During the session, I suddenly remembered my first conscious memory, and it involved my dad

LEARN IT,
BE IT,
LEAD IT

pulling my dad off of me, along with my mom, but I don't remember my aunt being there. I do remember the red- and-white can of Budweiser beer, which was my dad's drink of choice in his worst moments.

Within about two hours, I'd learned to tie my own shoes. I have a very specific way of tying them, not the bunny-ears style, but to this day I still tie them in the same way. If one of the strings comes undone, I go to pieces. For this reason, I'm very self-conscious about my appearance. For instance, Mike and I went on a cruise earlier this year, the first one we've been able to take since the beginning of the pandemic. While onboard one evening, we enjoyed a steak dinner together. I'll admit I was a little drunk at the steakhouse, which is rare for me since I don't drink anywhere unless it's on a cruise ship. A piece of steak fell on my shirt and I got a nice ketchup stain down my front.

No big deal for most people, but I lost it. I was crying. I was bawling because I would be walking out of the restaurant with this stain on my shirt. I can't stand to be embarrassed in any situation. It's something that's definitely stuck with me ever since I was little.

I've never smoked a cigarette. That's God's honest truth. I only drink when Mike and I are on a cruise. I hate alcohol because of what it did to my dad and growing up being targeted by its volcanic and violent effects on his temperament. So any drink I have is few and far between. I don't get drunk like normal people get drunk. I am diabetic, so it kind of flows right through my system. If Mike wakes up with a hangover, I'm usually the first out of bed after a night of steady drinking saying, "Let's go! Come on!" I turn on every light in the cabin, and he gets mad and throws a pillow at me. Drinking has always been a way to release some steam, but it can be done responsibly. Limited drinks on rare special occasions and no drugs. I haven't been in any other trouble besides writing bad checks.

For these reasons and others, I'm very much my mother's baby, being her first, and I always will be. Mike knows not to pick up the phone and call mom and say anything critical about me because he knows he'll be on the phone for the next hour with her just trying to digest whatever she might say in my defense. This protectiveness has always been her *modus operandi,* even when I was first married to Mandy, my high school sweetheart.

Right before Mandy was about to walk down the aisle, my mom decided to pick a fight and politely reminded my future ex-wife, "There will only be one Mrs. Byrd and you will never be the one." Without missing a beat, Mandy said, "Well, I am now." I was so embarrassed. People literally had to pull my mom out of the room!

My father is 74 years old now, and my mom is 65, and it's safe to say that time has given them the wisdom, understanding, and temperance they lacked when I was growing up. Perhaps my dad saw the light when my mother threatened to divorce him at one point. He simply can't live

LEARN IT,
BE IT,
LEAD IT

without her. My dad is a big ol' teddy bear now, and we have a great relationship. Mike and I even enjoy spending the holidays with them, but the fact is that my dad couldn't live without my mom. He doesn't clean, cook, or do laundry-nothing. He's very Southern in that way where he's the main breadwinner and mom takes care of all the daily household chores. If something happened to my mom today, my dad would go within 30 days. It's more than a prediction, but a fact that even my siblings and I have come to accept as his inevitable fate.

My parents met through some mutual friends in Muncie and they quickly fell in love, married, and had me all before my mother was in her twenties. They met at seventeen, married the following year, and I was the result of their union. I have two younger brothers. Scottie joined the

family two-and-a-half years after me, and Jerred arrived

about a decade after Scottie.

I'm still close to my family and brothers, although Scottie has had his fair share of troubles in recent years. Scottie was always Dad's favorite. He still is to this day, and that's just the way it is. As I said, Scottie has run into a lot of trouble in the recent past and dad has always come to his rescue. It's fair to say that my folks have always been there for my brothers and me when the going got tough. But, of course, speaking from my own experience, I have only myself to blame for the strife that would follow.

LEARN IT, BE IT, LEAD IT

Jerred works for the State of Indiana, and he and his wife have a two-and-a-half-year-old little girl. When not working for the state, Jerred is a semi-pro wrestler for Delaware County Championship Wrestling or DDCW, a family-friendly pro wrestling organization, where he wrestles under the name Mike King. We both look alike; similar build, but Jerred's bigger than me in most respects. He's 6'3" and 300 lbs, while I'm 5' 11" and 270 lbs. Scottie is just as tall, 6'1", lanky, and half of Jerred's weight. Then there's me, your typical Midwest build and stature, pretty unassuming.

Growing up together, we always had everything we ever needed to keep us entertained. We always took family vacations together. At home, we always had something to do or recklessly ride around on, like a three-wheeler or a dirt bike. During the wintertime, we would pull a sled behind the three-wheeler, and my brothers and I would try to throw each other off, as we slid across our family's sprawling acreage, which was adjacent to the family farm. Plenty of room for boys to be boys and do stupid stuff.

That was my childhood in a nutshell-boys being boy. Every Thursday after school, I was expected to mow the lawn, and I remember the countless crabapple fights my brothers and I had on the riding lawn mower. Let's just say that crabapples make excellent projectiles as you mow over them. My dad would be there, too, lording over all these antics. If anything broke down, like the belt on the tractor, or the weed eater stopped working, even if I hadn't touched

LEARN IT,
BE IT,
LEAD IT

it, it was automatically my fault. There was no letup from my dad's strict rules. I had a TV in my room, a luxury then, but my father took it out in the driveway and busted it when I came home with bad grades. For each C that we got, it was half an hour's worth of homework and each D was an hour's worth of homework.

My father's way of showing love and affection was through money and gifts. When the Nintendo Entertainment System first came on the market, my father got us one for Christmas, and Scottie and I would play Super Mario Bros. Even though we weren't really close, we were close growing up. We would go to our aunt's house on Christmas Eve and we would come home for our family Christmas together. The entire living room floor would be covered with presents. My folks would set out the gifts right before we left to go to my aunt's house, so when we got back home, there would be literally no room to walk because there were so many presents.

We also had a willow tree in the back of our home, which made for the worst switches, perfect for my mom's occasional fits of discipline on us boys. I remember going into a department store called Zayre, which was a Midwest chain, kind of like Big Lots on crack. Anytime she took us boys to Zayre's, my mom would pull a stick off the willow tree, fashion it into a switch and place it on the dashboard in the car. Before we got to the store, she would tell us, "Don't ask for anything." She never had to use it on us, but

LEARN IT, BE IT, LEAD IT

it was always a threat and we knew she meant it. After all, she loved us, too.

However, we weren't above being spanked in front of both God and man. Once about the time I was sixteen, Jerred really wanted a toy in Wal-Mart and begged mom repeatedly to get it for him. She told him "no" twice, and by the third time he asked, he was getting his butt spanked in the parking lot. Some lady looked at mom inflicting corporal punishment and said, "Ma'am, you can't do that in public." "You're next," my mom snapped back. I'll never forget it, and that's who my mom is-crazy, a little nuts, but it all comes from a place of love. We always had fun, especially when my dad wasn't around.

Muncie is a very blue-collar town, and when it came to white-collar crime, which I will be convicted of much later in this story, I had to shut the door on all of it to forge my own destiny.

2

HEAVEN & HELL

School was hell for me-a living hell that I had to accept with very little say over. Despite this, I was surrounded by a stern, yet loving support system.

With my family, my brothers and I could be wild, but always within the bounds of the rules. At school, it was a much different picture, with forces seemingly beyond my control. Whether that was from the school culture or Muncie society as a whole, my peers always found ways of singling me out and torturing me just for being me.

By the time I'd reached the third grade, ideas about the appropriate levels of instruction at school had been turned upside down. For some reason, the teachers decided to "dumb down" their instruction so that a third-grade classroom could be taught more like a second-grade classroom, and so on.

Mrs. Barber was my third-grade teacher at Grissom Elementary and a large part of the reason I was held back a grade and didn't end up graduating with classmates my own

LEARN IT, BE IT, LEAD IT

age. She had put me out in the hallway a couple of times for talking during class or whatever-pretty normal stuff. But I was persistent. After about a week of me talking out of turn, she decided to call my mom in for a conference about my behavior. Luckily, on that particular day, my dad was at work. For her small stature and diminutive size, nothing sets my mom off like other people trying to "parent" her own children for her. As Mrs. Barber explained my problematic classroom behavior to my mom, the next thing I know, here comes the principal and the vice-principal storming down the hallway. I stood there and watch the hullabaloo my mom stirred up, and before I knew it, my mom essentially flipped the tables on Mrs. Barber and the principal for constantly removing me from the classroom. Mrs. Barber had the final say-she said I was disruptive, unruly, and I needed to be held back a grade. After that decision was agreed upon, I found myself the object of derision by a string of hyper- masculine bullies. I had to learn to stand on my own two feet. I couldn't rely on my mother's protection as I once had. One of my classmates was a kid by the name of Gary.

I'll never forget this guy. He had a brother named Mike and their father worked with my dad at the forge. It just goes to show how closed-off Muncie was-everyone knew everybody. In the case of Gary, he knew me too well and made my life a living hell from that point on until I graduated. He would tease me, bully me, and even chase me from school back to my house every day after class. If I saw him again today,

I wouldn't hesitate to run him over with my car. He was an evil, nasty, and mean kid, and today, I can only imagine he lives an evil, nasty, and mean life. I look him up on Facebook before I fly back into town, and the last time I checked he worked for the cable company. So yeah, *definitely* evil.

I'll never forget this one moment in the fifth grade. We were in Sex Ed class, where everyone was laughing, snickering, watching an educational video, and the whole nine yards. There was Gary with his dick out, just having fun, waving it around underneath his desk. Maybe he had some kind of latent homosexual feelings, but I don't think I was meant to see it, because he was showing it to all the girls. Still, I'll remember Gary and his member until the day I die. Regardless, I became the target of Gary and his friends' anger and malice, especially in regard to my sexuality, which I didn't fully comprehend myself. They seemed to know that I was gay before I'd even come out as gay. They certainly seemed to know me better than I knew myself, but looking back, maybe things were going on in their own lives I wasn't fully aware of. But they all knew me and Gary started it.

I may have been too young at the time to fully appreciate what was going on with my sexuality, but by the time I'd

reach fifth grade, J.R. brought it all into perspective for me.

Starting in elementary school about the time I was twelve, throughout our time at Wilson Middle School, and up to the point we graduated from high school and he moved

LEARN IT, BE IT, LEAD IT

away, J.R. became one of my closest friends. My first sexual experiences were with him. No one ever targeted J.R. for being gay, but they certainly did me, so when we when started hanging out, the assumption that I was gay by association seemed to buzz throughout the hallways at school.

J.R. and I are still friends on Facebook, but we really don't talk. Still, the fact we grew up together has made our friendship more enduring. After I was released from prison,

J.R. and his family would come to visit me while I was in the work-release program, and even took me to church on Sundays. I still love his family to death; they're like a second family to me.

In this way and others, school was like a daily death wish for me. Although I had supportive, overbearing parents, I had a good home and a very tight-knit circle of about two or

three friends, including J.R. and Curtisa, who lived across

the street from us and became close friends with Mandy at beauty school years later. Our lives have diverged and we

only connect on Facebook infrequently, but J.R., Curtisa,

and I are still friends. Along with my family, they made my childhood much more tolerable, and the fact that I survived it somehow is a testament to their friendship. But if I ever see Gary again, I swear, he's roadkill.

The only other place where I could escape the harsh realities of growing up in a conservative little town like Muncie was in the sanctuary of religion. I've experienced a broad scope of evangelical Christianity. I was raised in the

LEARN IT, BE IT, LEAD IT

Baptist church, then the Pentecostal, then the Episcopal church, but that didn't seem so strange then, considering that in Muncie, there are more churches than there are cornfields.

Initially, my family attended a Southern Baptist Church when I was little. Then we switched to a Pentecostal Apostolic Church, although you'd be hard-pressed to tell the difference in worship styles between the two. I was never one to run up and down the aisles screaming the name of Jesus. That was not me. To watch ladies faint and the preacher pray over them, speaking in tongues, and to have the cross put on my head and the anointing with oil didn't appeal to me. It wasn't something that I could get into.

J.R. and I had grown up together, and by the time I was in my early teens, I began attending the Indianapolis International Church of Christ, or ICOC, with J.R., since he was already attending worship services there. I went with him and his family and together we drove from Muncie to Indianapolis, which is about an hour-and-ten-minute drive, every Wednesday and Sunday, and then sometimes every other Friday. For a time, I enjoyed going to church. But like so many churches that hide behind the veneer of a wholesome, family-orientated congregation, the sense of belonging I longed for most within the church eventually betrayed those feelings through scandal and hypocrisy. In short, ICOC was a cult.

LEARN IT, BE IT, LEAD IT

ICOC is an evangelical, non-denominational megachurch with tens of thousands of congregants the world over. It has been around for well over a century, since its inception in Boston. By 1993, the Indianapolis branch off of ICOC alone had at least 1,000 members, of which I was one. The teachings and beliefs of ICOC might seem mundane by today's standards, including accepting the Bible as absolute truth and a guide for living, doing good works, and confession as a means of evangelism.

Beyond that, according to the church leadership, the only path to salvation was to essentially conform to the rest of the group. Fall in line, or you're out. Eventually, church leaders Kip McKean and Ed Powers splintered over several controversial issues within the church, including interpretation of doctrine and mandatory tithing, but it was encouraging college students to abandon school and join the ministry that caused the scandal, to the point that it attracted the national news media. Powers eventually left ICOC to start a new offshoot church in Los Angeles. The Indianapolis branch split into two new branches, the divides were so deep between church leaders.

When I really got into the worship service and the doctrine of ICOC, I was assigned a discipler named Sean. A discipler is somebody that, before you're baptized into the church, you tell all your sins to and that sort of thing- kind of like the person that you go to for guidance, who is employed by the church. Wednesday night is Bible Study

LEARN IT,
BE IT,
LEAD IT

night at ICOC, and that was the night where I would tell Sean all my sins, which included any secret desires related to my sexuality. If you masturbated that week, they wanted to know about it. Homosexuality, in the eyes of the ICOC, was something that was "bad" and should be put away and left alone. Not the most healthy approach for a young man like myself who was just trying to figure out his own way through the hellscape of one's teenage years.

By the time I was a Junior at Southside High School, about 1993-'94, the church leadership scandal had erupted, and even my parents had had enough with ICOC. The issue was the mandatory donations, amongst other contentions. We were all asked to give donations and if you did not give a certain amount, you were looked upon poorly as if you could not be fruitful or prosperous. Your tree did not bear fruit. The disciplers already knew everything about you, including who you worked for and how much you made, in addition to any sexual sins. That's when it really hit home for me, that asking people for spare change was the real test of your devotion. During worship, they passed around these blue velvet bags that more closely resembled Crown Royal whiskey bags, but with no logo or lettering on them. We were told it was for ongoing missionary work, including the establishment of a new branch of the church somewhere in Africa.

A toxic combination of greed and religion will make anyone do pretty crazy stuff. As teens in the church, searching

LEARN IT, BE IT, LEAD IT

for a sense of belonging and identity, we needed to fill up so many bags and give so much of our paychecks to the ICOC. I remember the scandal involving Ed Powers because it got everyone's attention, and J.R.'s parents were big in the church and well-connected with the leadership. In fact, I remember sitting at the top of the stairs at J.R.'s house and listening to his parents downstairs discuss leaving ICOC as it was becoming two different churches. The kicker is, that both of those churches, Rise Up and City Center in Indianapolis, are still going strong today.

When my parents saw the news report about ICOC and

Ed Powers, their dislike for my church family intensified. They believed it was a cult, and I remember talking them down and reassuring them that it wasn't, since that was a part of what we were trained to do during Bible Studies at the church. In some sense, I, along with J.R. and many other young men and women, was brainwashed into thinking these things, all in the name of defending some unethical practices within the church.

For me, ICOC was life. I was not involved in extracurricular or outside activities at school. Greetings were expressed as hugs at church. There were no handshakes. It was all hugs. Having the father that I had, receiving that sense of touch, that sense of belonging, that sense of being there for somebody, actually meant a lot to me whenever I went to church.

LEARN IT,
BE IT,
LEAD IT

Everybody was alike at ICOC, so you can understand the sense of togetherness and safety in numbers that comes from that. No matter who you were, you belonged. To be out of ICOC's favor and not follow their guidelines was asking to be excised from the church. Why not want to be loved by doing what you're told at one point in your life? I think that was the draw for me. By the time I'd married Mandy at the end of our teenage years, her dislike for the church and my mother's dislike for Mandy was enough that I stopped going to ICOC altogether. She didn't trust J.R. either.

During my teenage years, I realized I existed between two worlds-one, a hellish nightmare where I was persecuted just for being gay, and the other, heaven, where I felt a sense of optimism and community beyond my own family that I longed for. Neither world was meant to last.

3

LEARNING THE SYSTEM

came from a home where you work nonstop. You worked to better your own life and the lives of your family.

A strong work ethic in our home was something that was instilled early. I have been working since I was old enough to fourteen-and-a-half years old to be exact if that tells you anything. My dad always believed that hard work is its own reward and part of learning. We weren't handed anything growing up, even though my brothers and I were frequently spoiled. Even though I came from a upper- middle-class family, I worked hard for what was mine, and now in retirement, I can say the success that I found in my own career in property management is the result of those long-standing values.

Muncie is renowned for the number of fast-food restaurants within the city limits. At one point in the mid- 90s, even *Time* magazine reported that there were at least five fast-food restaurants for every resident in Muncie. Every fast food joint you can possibly think of is located

LEARN IT, BE
IT, LEAD IT

down McGalliard Street. Pizza King has some of the best pizza in the world; a must-stop place to eat if you're ever in town, but I made my dough in those days soaked in steam, sweat, and grease, awash in the brilliant yellow glow of the golden arches-McDonald's.

I first started working at McDonald's at 364 South Madison Avenue. That particular location has been in operation since McDonald's first arrived in Muncie. Speedee, a cutesy character with a hamburger-shaped head and a chef's outfit, greeted me every day with his characteristic wink and smile. An early McDonald's ad campaign in the late 1950s that preceded Ronald McDonald, the Madison Avenue location has one of three remaining Speedee neon marquees left across the nation. You'd have to go to Wisconsin or Florida to see Speedee anywhere else.

When I first started working for McDonald's, you could only work three-and-a-half-hour shifts, which I worked in the drive-thru area. Things started off well. The first day I began working, some upset lady threw a tray with Coke and Dr. Pepper at me, she was so angry. I was immediately ready to quit until my manager at the time told me to make something of myself and grow a pair, which I did.

Eventually, the hard work and dedication earned me multiple promotions and by the time I'd graduated high school, I was one of the youngest managers in the entirety of the McOpCo Corporation. I worked for McDonald's well beyond the city limits, too. After I was married and moved to

LEARN IT, BE IT, LEAD IT

Florida, I served as a manager at Coral Springs, and when I returned to Indiana, I also took up the same responsibilities at New Castle. It was a great McDonald's to work for. In Coral Springs, there was an old Marine sergeant who taught me a lot while I was working there for about three months, then Mandy and I came back to Indiana and I started at the McDonald's in New Castle. At that point, J.R. and I reconnected on MySpace.

It wasn't all "Food, Folks n' Fun," of course. Being a manager wasn't the easiest job title, especially in a place where there's a near-constant stream of customers. Fortunately, I very rarely had to fire an employee who didn't make the grade behind the counter. I can count on one hand the number of employees I gave the ax to, including one guy who had stolen $50 from the cash till after it had come up short one evening.

Over the years, I've

completed every conceivable manager training. McDonald's offered-Intermediate Operations, Basic Shift Management, you name it. The only height of the internal McDonald's hierarchy I didn't reach was Hamburger University, located at the global corporate headquarters in Chicago, which is where potential restaurant managers, mid-level managers, and owner-operators are trained and earn a degree in the art of all things hamburger. When I moved to Las Vegas, I still worked for McDonald's.

In 2004, the real estate market wasn't quite what it is now, so I stuck with what I knew until a better opportunity presented

LEARN IT, BE IT, LEAD IT

itself. While working at McDonald's could be relentless at times, I learned some important life lessons that allowed me to be a model and example to others.

I loved work. I loved going to work. One lesson I learned during my time at McDonald's is a no-brainer: never give up. It only takes one tray full of soda pop being hurled at you to appreciate that lesson. Another is the importance of learning people skills-know what people want, delivering on promises, and do not suffer people who lie, cheat, and steal to get their way. They will only keep lying to you if you keep them around. Above all, in a fast-paced environment, be you. I'll admit that I struggled with this the first eighteen years of my life, trying to better understand myself while keeping my head above water. All these lessons would serve me well, including living in the throngs of matrimony, behind steel bars, and in the dry air of the high desert in the years that followed.

4

THE THRILL OF IT ALL

always knew I was gay, but it wasn't until I was in Junior High that I began acting on this exciting new sense of

myself. I was probably twelve or thirteen when **J.R.** and

I started playing around. He was always at the bottom. The first time we explored our sexuality with one another was unforgettable, to say the least, and maybe for the wrong reasons because he was scared half to death. We thought we were going to have to tell his parents because he bled a little bit down there.

Within about a year, our activities graduated from just oral into the actual sexual act. In some ways, it felt completely natural-boys playing with each other like boys normally do. You have a sleepover, and you play with one another. "Oh, you're bigger than I am." "Oh no, you're bigger than me." That sort of thing. I think that's how boys are. J.R. and I continued this with one another well into high school, even while we attended ICOC together, and well past the point

LEARN IT, BE IT, LEAD IT

Mandy and I were married. She never knew. My discipler and everyone at ICOC never knew either.

On the Fourth of July, 1995, I married my high school sweetheart, Mandy. Mandy and I had our first-grade picture taken together. That's how long we were together before we'd even gotten married. Our romantic infatuation with one another was interrupted in places by occasional break-ups over the years, but it was always destined to be between us no matter what I did.

Both Mandy and I grew up in very Christian households, so we were raised to adhere to the same set of values and beliefs. I don't hate Mandy. I hate who she became, but I don't hate her for what she did later on when I was trying to elude the police over the bad checks. The writing was all over the wall, so to speak, where Mandy and I would be pitted against one another. Our divorce entailed a cat named Claribel that we got together. There are two pages in our divorce about this cat. During the divorce hearing, the judge asked, "How am I to divide this cat? I can't slice the thing in half and separate it between you two." The judge ruled that Mandy should take custody of the cat to avoid further conflict between us. Eventually, Mandy told me that poor Claribel had passed, or at least that's what she claimed. Mandy and I weren't always at odds with one another.

It was comforting to know that Mandy's father was gay. We were so much alike that I could have been his biological child. At one point, Mandy and I tried to have kids together,

LEARN IT,
BE IT,
LEAD IT

but couldn't. In fact, she was told not to have kids by a doctor, but now she has two boys with a different man, of course. They say that you always marry someone like your dad. Well, she did and now she's married to a guy who looks like me, but he's a complete one-eighty turn from who I am as a person. So good for them. About once every five years, we say "Hi" to each other on Facebook. I'm not a total jerk, even to my ex-wife.

I wasn't ready to get married. In fact, at seventeen, I'd moved out of my folks' house and into a one-bedroom apartment waiting to get married to Mandy. Most everyone my age had moved out of the house before graduation, so it didn't seem so odd then. I wasn't aware of it, but during that time, I was learning just to be me. I was learning who I was. JR. had come over a couple of times to "visit" me, but I don't think Mandy ever knew about it. It was a really weird, uncertain time being out on my own. A part of me also loved the sense of independence that came from living out from under my parents' thumbs. Don't get me wrong. When the check-writing started, that's when I got into trouble-a *lot* of trouble.

During my time at McDonald's in Muncie, even though I was making great money, I was writing bad checks. If you've ever had a checking account, no doubt you've written bad checks, maybe, complete with overdraft charges or returned check fees as well. I wasn't just writing a bad check here or there, I wrote many bad checks.

LEARN IT, BE IT, LEAD IT

I began writing bad checks at the age of seventeen, and this habit continued up until I was arrested at nineteen. I won't say I have any regrets, because of course I do. Everyone does. Even though my conviction has since vanished after Judge Wolf wiped my record clean in 2020, it's still a part of my life I know very well.

I've always had a curious mind. I love to be inquisitive, to take things apart and figure out how things work, even if I'm not the most coordinated person. To write a bad check, I had to learn the banking system and the ins and outs of how checking accounts work. This was my method: I would open a checking account at a bank. I would then get their counter checks and go to another bank and write another check to that bank using the counter checks. Then eventually the account balance would accrue and I would withdraw all the money out of the bank.

It was an adrenaline rush to go into a bank and open an account with $2,500 and wait three days for that check to clear in another bank account. I always looked for a bank that did not use a check scan or pulled an Experian report to open a new checking account. I knew that roughly three-to-seven business days later, the check would come back and bounce into that bank account. Within the first three days, the bank would release the $2,500 in funds. What did I do on the third day? I went up and got the $2,500 dollars out. Now that the check was bouncing in the one bank, I would take that 2,500 dollars and go open

LEARN IT,
BE IT,
LEAD IT

a new account or go float another check to another bank. With this method, at one point, I had at least seventeen bank accounts total.

I bought a Mercedes with a bad check. You name it, I did it. I bought a bright purple suit jacket at this upscale clothing store called New York & Company in the Muncie Mall. Try to imagine the most '90s suit you could buy- in all the '90s colors, with a mustard yellow shirt and bright purple jacket, dark pants, and pearl button cover with inlaid little rhinestones. That was my get-up to go places or go out somewhere. It would've looked clowning by today's standards, but it didn't feel that way.

I felt like Leonardo DiCaprio's character in the film *Catch Me If Thu Can*. Writing bad checks allowed me to lead the lifestyle I imagined for myself. It let me buy better clothes and other stupid stuff when that money could have gone to a better cause instead of being spent by an idiotic kid who didn't know any better. No one was there to stop me or tell me, no, and even though I knew right from wrong and knew what I was doing was wrong, it didn't stop me from doing it. It didn't feel wrong, because I learned how to work a system to my advantage that most people are ignorant of, or take for granted.

True, my bad check debts were sent to a collection agency, but no big deal. The TeleCheck logo, which was a small sticker business placed on their doors to show they would process any checks electronically, was the golden ticket to

LEARN IT, BE IT, LEAD IT

write another bad check. Also, when I moved to Florida, many bank clerks there couldn't read an Indiana driver's license anyway. Checks written across state lines were processed differently. Yet another opportunity to defraud the banks and walk away with all of God's money. The fact that I was effectively working a seemingly foolproof system was a thrill of **it** for me. Add on top of that the sensation of not getting caught, and you might understand what led me down this self-destructive path in my late teens.

Even though I was making good money at McDonald's, in my mind, it was being able to do what I wanted, when I wanted, and knowing how the banking system rotated on its axis. I took great satisfaction in it. It was as though I was able to say, "I know how it works and I beat your fucking system. Fuck you." That was the thrill for me.

I believe there's ample published research to suggest that many bad check writers, myself included, suffer from a bipolar or obsessive-compulsive disorder. Many of us were diagnosed with ADHD. It's how our brains are wired, although old habits die hard. Even now, out of prison, every year or so, I get a new car. Mike actually hates when I do this, and it's not because I need a new car, but it's the thrill of getting a loan and haggling with somebody over the prince. It's the thrill of having a shiny new car parked in front of the house and everybody looking at it as they pass by knowing what you have.

LEARN IT, BE IT, LEAD IT

There are not a lot of people out there like me. I'm very materialistic. Mike once said to me, "I hate that about you. If you want something, you're going to make it happen." Yeah, I will. Just the other day, we went to a new lender to start looking at building another house. We've talked about building another home for years. This will be our eighth property. For me, it's always been about the thrill of getting the ball rolling. In my book, today is always the day to make magic happen.

Do I have regrets? Absolutely. But did it make me who I

became? Yes. I made a lot of money to be as young as I was and to go out and write checks and stuff made absolutely no sense in retrospect. I think that it was the thrill more than anything and the adrenaline rush to see what I could do or what I could buy and work the banking system of the mid-90s to my advantage. To have a nice car or nice clothes, something to show for it, only added to my sense of pride in having committed the crime. Sooner or later, I knew I would be doing the time.

5

BAD CHECKS

Inevitably, I was caught. When all the charges were stacked against me, there were fifteen felonies and over 50 misdemeanors. This is probably the most painful part of my story, personally, and it's hard to relive these moments

in my memory. They give me nightmares.

I knew it was coming. I just didn't know when. I had written a check to a bank called the National Bank of Detroit, or NBD Bank. It's no longer around; Chase eventually bought them out, but the check I wrote with NBD bank is the one I pled guilty on. It was called fraud on a financial institution, which was a Class C felony. At that time, they graded the classes of felonies D, C, B, and A. A was the worst. D was like a misdemeanor. Usually, most attorneys will plead down Class D felonies to a misdemeanor.

When I realized that the jig was up, the cops were already looking for me. The police came and knocked on the door of my parent's home, the dream home they'd purchased together while I was still in high school after we'd relocated to

Albany, and asked where I was. I remember calling my dad, who explained to me the dire situation as it was unfolding.

"Chris, whatever you do, don't open the door," he said. "If they are looking for you and you're not there, they'll eventually leave." By that time, my parents had already hired an attorney, but he turned out to be a shiesty fucker. He was disbarred for drugs, alcohol, and hiring prostitutes, so eventually, he was replaced.

I left Mandy by herself, got in the car, and drove to my aunt's house in Kentucky that very night to lay low for a while. No one knew where I was except for my parents and of course, they weren't going to say anything. It was Mandy who turned me in when I was on the run, which was the most heartbreaking thing to endure. I never meant to put her through so much pain having to make that choice either. My aunt Sharon lived in Kentucky, and she still does. It's the same place where my mother was born, on a mountaintop in Versailles, Kentucky just off Lillard's Ferry Way Road. I called Mandy to check and make sure that everything was OK, but the authorities had beaten me to them. Mandy was told if she saw an unknown number on the caller ID to let the detectives know. The number I was calling from was unfamiliar to her, so after a warrant was issued to get the information on the caller ID, they quickly found out it was

under my aunt's name.

I went to a car auction with my aunt that evening, and on the way back, my uncle called, "Sharon, he has been all over the scanner. You might not want to go home." So I got down low in the backseat and told my aunt to take me to the nearest hotel. She even paid for the night that I spent there. I told her that if I was arrested, or something were to happen, I didn't want it to be at their home or in front of the kids and that I would call her to check in the next morning. Later that night, I heard a knock on the hotel room door.

I told myself not to answer it, thinking I'd listen to my dad's instructions on this one. Don't answer the door, you idiot. Too late; the police let themselves in the room and the next thing I know, I was taken into custody and booked in a jail near Frankfort, just outside of Lexington. Game over.

I waited ten days in jail for the Muncie sheriff to come and pick me up once I had waived my rights, which I did. While I was awaiting extradition in jail, I was raped. One day, I was taking a shower, getting ready for a visit from Aunt Sharon, and this big, humongous Black guy stepped into this tiny one-person shower I was scrubbing up in.

"What the fuck are you doing, dude?" I shouted. He didn't waste a second turning me around and showing me who the boss was.

Now, I'm not going to say I didn't enjoy it, because I didn't know before that I would like this new, sudden and violent experience. He was a bigger guy, and it hurt for a little bit after that. I never reported it, but I described the incident to the probation officer who came in and interviewed me. That testimony was given to the judge, and it was included in the

LEARN IT, BE IT, LEAD IT

court records during my sentencing as a mitigating factor, as it was called, in hopes of somehow lessening my sentence for having been brutalized in custody.

On the tenth day in jail, the Delaware County Sheriff arrived to pick me up and I was returned to Muncie. From that point on, I never left jail for almost two years. I was charged in June 1996. On each of the 52 misdemeanors for writing bad checks, I faced a fine of up to 250 dollars per check and one-to-three years in prison plus restitution for each of those checks as well. I think I had ten or twelve felony checks, and those were the checks the District Attorney decided to file against me when I was charged.

My parent's dream home was next door to Jim Davis, the creator of Garfield the Cat. They lost that home defending me from the courts. They actually sold it so I wouldn't go to prison and they helped me pay my attorney fees. Every time I bring up any of Scottie's troubles or my dad ends up paying for anything, the loss of that house is normally brought up and hung over my head, as a reminder of the price that was paid so I wouldn't have to suffer a harsher sentence than the one I was to receive.

After my initial lawyer was scandalized and disbarred, Robert Beymer took over his office. Robert was a little short, stout, bald-headed man with black glasses who wore nice suits and cowboy boots. He's since passed on. I was surprised when I met him for the very first time since I thought my dad was going to hire Mick Alexander, the

LEARN IT,
BE IT,
LEAD IT

a most prominent attorney in Delaware County and probably Indiana at that time. He defended murderers, rapists, and drug dealers-all kinds of criminals. Representing the state was a man named Lou Denney, who also long since passed. At one point, Mick, Robert, and Lou ended up working in the same attorney's office together, and Lou had also once represented Scottie in court.

In front of the judge, it turned out I was in capable hands, and Robert was able to plead all the charges against me down to one Class C felony, misdemeanors included. My attorney would later make the case that writing some bad checks isn't the worst crime one could commit and that I didn't deserve the sentence the law said I should receive. However, as I mentioned earlier, a white-collar crime in a blue-collar town is looked down upon.

At my sentencing in December 1997, I received five years. In Indiana, as long as you're a good inmate and well-behaved, you could potentially get out in two-and-a-half years. The judge was fair, and while I didn't get the ten-day credit for the time I spent in Kentucky, I was credited with time served for being in the Delaware County Jail, where I was kept for almost a year.

In Muncie, if you commit a blue-collar crime, hell, you'd go out, have one too many drinks at the bar, get pulled over, get a DUI, even do some meth, and not go to jail. That's what the authorities expect. They don't expect somebody to walk through their doors, take advantage of the system

LEARN IT, BE IT, LEAD IT

and know how a system works and not go to jail. It doesn't happen. They were going to make an example out of me.

6

BEHIND BARS

By the time I was 21 years old, I'd spent a total of two years in prison. Since I had good behavior behind bars, I was let out six months early. My Department of Corrections number was #971155, which means that I got my DOC number in the 97th year, the 11th month, and I was the 55th prisoner in the Indiana DOC. I began serving my sentence in Muncie and then eventually I was transferred to Indianapolis for work release and lived in the outside dormitory. Even though I was incarcerated, I was barely an hour and a half from my folk's house, but the majority of the sentence was spent in jail, which believe it or not is a lot more strict than prison is. You wouldn't think so, but it is.

Jail is much stricter and more regimented than prison. Jail is what you see on TV. Once you hit prison, in the first 30 days with the general population, even though I'd committed a white-collar crime, the corrections officers try to figure out how bad of a felon you actually are. It's a scary

LEARN IT, BE IT, LEAD IT

a place to be. At first, you think you'll be living comfortably amongst the white-collar inmates, but you get sent to general lock-up regardless. Everyone, there is scared half to death or you're just a kid like I was at nineteen years old that didn't have a clue what was going on or what to do. News from home or anywhere else outside the jail was hard to come by. My parents wrote me letters, so I was writing letters home back and forth, and I wasn't allowed any telephone calls, so I had to say everything I wanted to say in those letters.

At first, I shared a cell with a guy who had stabbed his wife to death. God's honest truth, I sucked him off on the floor of the jail cell. I also shared the same jail cell with a Black guy, but I never did anything sexual with him. I think he was there for drug dealing. But the guy I gave the blowjob to get moved to another cell by the third night I was there. He was considered a more volatile criminal for stabbing his wife than someone who'd written some bad checks.

In jail, it was common to share your cell with another inmate, but as a trustee, which I was, you're given a cell to yourself. You're trusted for several reasons, including good behavior or the non-violent nature of your crime, so you're not as fiercely monitored as the other inmates. You're helping out, staying busy, and doing chores around the jail, and for your efforts, you're given your own cell. While in jail, I was a trustee for almost a year in Delaware County. I was given the responsibility of working in the laundry room. They gave me loads of laundry. I did the

SO

LEARN IT,
BE IT,
LEAD IT

laundry and distributed fresh linens and uniforms back to my fellow inmates.

I was also assigned to kitchen duty. I had to get up at 3:30 in the morning and worked for a good portion of the day cooking food and cleaning up afterward. Later, when I returned to my cell, I was allowed to take a shower every day. The other guys weren't always allowed to, but since I worked hard in the kitchen, I was given other little luxuries like being able to watch a movie late into the night.

This went on for about a year until I was sent to Pendleton Correctional Facility just outside Indianapolis, where they categorized you based on your behavior and the severity of the crime. So let's say you're a murderer. You either go behind the wall at Pendleton or you go up to Wabash Valley Correctional Facility. Death row is at Wabash now. I don't think Pendleton has a death row anymore, but it's imposing enough since it looks like a castle. It was one of the oldest prisons in Indiana.

But if you're a white-collar criminal like I was with no other prior record, they decided I was a good candidate for the outside dormitory. Some of those guys had been to prison once or twice for domestic violence or a DUI that resulted in someone's death, but if you had no prior convictions, they'd consider you for better accommodations.

At first, I was scared, but even the most intelligent and resourceful individuals are capable of adapting to new surroundings. Even so, you become "prisonized." You accept

LEARN IT, BE
IT, LEAD IT

the conditions in which you live and develop a consistent routine that keeps you safe and out of trouble. It works like this: You get up in the morning. You play cards. You do your laundry. You do this. You do that. It is a very regimented lifestyle behind bars, but in this way, you stay safe.

I got into a few books, mostly mysteries, right before I was transferred to prison. I would read a whole novel in one day because I was in lockdown. They try to prepare you for what prison life is like. And so, they would let half the guys out for the first half of the day, and the other half out for the back half of the day. So you learn a way of life. I'll never forget undergoing that transition into prison and no matter who you were, you got undressed, you took a shower, and then you got this stuff thrown on you just like they do on the HBO show *Oz*. I'd never even seen *Oz,* but that's exactly how it was. They throw this powder on you to control lice and other vermin that looks and smells just like Ajax Cleaner, and then it took another shower to wash it off. Jail is not scary and I tell those people that think jail is scary that it's nothing compared to prison, because even though you're in the outside dormitory and it's a dorm, it's still a dorm setting. It's older than dirt with no AC and you're just waiting to go to work-release. So you're sitting there and you don't even know the name of the guy sleeping next to you, nor what they did to get there, and it wasn't always bad checks either. They are there because they beat the shit out of somebody and were convicted of manslaughter. Even

LEARN IT,
            BE IT,
           LEAD IT

though it was violent, it's their first time, so where do they get put? The outside dormitory, where they could be your bunkmate above you or below you. Strangers are sleeping next to you, and it's as disconcerting as you might think.

At least in a jail cell, more than likely it's probably going to be about the same kind of criminal that you are because they're not going to put a violent criminal in with a person like me. They don't want me to get shanked or murdered or a violent criminal going ballistic on me. So jails are very different from prisons. Prisons are on lockdown 24/7, and you spend all of your time in C block, which was a trustee block, where the lowest-ranking felons on the planet lived alongside you. On various occasions, I was moved to D block or O block waiting to learn if I was going to the outside dorm.

I was still young at this time, still inexperienced, and at one point, I fell and hit every branch of the dick tree on the way down. When I was transferred to O block, my cellmates and I had a blast, freely and frequently acting out our sexual impulses. It was the biggest sexual experience I'd ever had. When I finally ended up in the outside dorm, I met Eric. He had a fiancée and two kids, but for him, it was all about the physical act of sex. For me, it was all about emotional attachment. It was a way to make things go a little bit smoother and a little bit faster to pass the time. At least I knew who I was and had a better sense of myself. Everybody knew Eric and I took a shower together every single night. It was the weirdest thing in the world. Nobody

LEARN IT, BE IT, LEAD IT

ever said anything because it was an open shower. For me, being with Eric was feeling a sense of belonging, having fun, and making my time go faster, while fully embracing the man I'd become.

Aside from sex, I passed the time learning how to play Spades and Hearts. I watched a lot of tv and everyone in the cell block got a kick out of watching *jerry Springer* together. Most of what I did in jail was play cards every night with the same guys, no matter what was going on. You would think these guys would get mad and be bad sports with each other, but it wasn't about that. Everybody needed something to do and we would sit there for hours on end until it was time to go to bed every night of the week.

While I was in jail, Mandy filed for divorce. We had discussed it previously, but one day I was brought out of my cell and rode the elevator down to the courtroom where Mandy was waiting along with her attorney, a woman named Mary Louise Baker. While she has since passed away, Mary Louise was a notorious man-hater. She despised every man who walked the face of the earth. Even if you were a woman with a dick, she hated you. If you had a single molecule of testosterone in your system, she hated you.

Had Mandy just handed me the papers, I would've signed them without any hesitation, but nope. There were Mandy, her mother, and Mary Louise on one side of the courtroom, while I was sitting there in chains with my parents seated behind me on the other side. Mandy didn't

LEARN IT,
BE IT,
LEAD IT

just want my balls in a vice, she wanted it all, which is why my parents were there. There was little I could do since I was in it for the long haul in jail. There were the financial burdens Mandy wanted restitution for, and then the nearly two pages about Claribel the cat, whom I mentioned earlier. It was the strangest divorce proceeding you can imagine.

Out from under Mandy's shadow, I felt certain now more than ever of my blossoming sexuality, of the man I'd become, to whom I was most attracted, so I decided that there was no better time than now to write the letter to my parents and tell them that I was gay. I apologized for causing them any sorrow or pain and told my mother how much I loved her.

I missed my family. Everybody misses their family. There was a point where I missed Mandy, but most of all, I missed my family. I also missed my grandmother's funeral. I think that was the biggest kicker for me. I had actually been approved to leave jail and attend grandma's funeral. I was a trustee, after all, and I was even allowed to wear street clothes. However, at the last minute, the supervisor took away the street clothes and wouldn't let me leave, so I never got a chance to say a final goodbye to her. That really kind of set the mood for what the rest of my time behind bars felt like. Privileges could be given and immediately taken away for the stupidest reasons. You never knew, which made life back then somewhat precarious and unpredictable beyond the normal daily routine. Loneliness is an especially cruel cellmate.

LEARN IT, BE
IT, LEAD IT

There's an old adage about honor amongst thieves, and it's really true, when you consider that some people make a career out of going to jail or remaining in jail, they become so indoctrinated and immersed in the prison culture that they become "prisonized," as I said earlier. It's all they've ever known. You don't know anything else, so you continue to go back. No one on the inside is showing you how to live on the outside. So the only thing you know is, "I got free food that comes to me every day. I have a job. I make a nickel an hour in the prison kitchen. I have a bed to sleep in. I might have air conditioning in the summertime and heat in the wintertime." Prison does nothing to prepare these guys to actually leave prison. They are only preparing them to come back. In essence, prison life prepares you to become a better criminal while you're inside, so the likelihood of becoming a repeat offender is only greater once you're released.

Remember, these guys normally don't have a family outside of prison, nor much of a life. They have nobody that comes up and visits them. If they do, it's their own cellmate-the guy that got away with the three murders but only got caught for one and talks about the three murders he got away with. So now, their cellmate is there for a DUI for six months and now knows how to kill somebody and get away with it.

Compare that to another guy that's been there for seven years and teaches his cellmate how to pay bills, cook meals, the facts of life, what's a good interest rate, and after seven

LEARN IT,
BE IT,
LEAD IT

years, his credits are wiped clean, and he's coming out with a fresh start, fresh credit, fresh everything. But the broken American prison system is such that they're not teaching him this stuff or rehabilitating him to re-enter society. They hand him a bus ticket, 75 dollars, and, "Get the fuck out." After his 75 dollars is gone and he's out on the streets, what do you think this guy is going to do? He's going to commit another crime and end up back where he started in jail. It's a self-defeating cycle.

Indiana has corn and prisons, nineteen prisons, both maximum and minimum security, to be exact. Why all these prisons? Why do you need prisons that are built to hold some of the worst criminals in the world? Wabash County has some of the most violent offenders in the United States. If you do your research or watch the news, you'll learn that prisons across the country are bursting at the seams, and prisoners are being transported across state lines to be incarcerated in other prisons outside the state where their crimes were committed. Taxpayers foot the bill for criminals to be locked up. Every day that you are there, every minute, every hour, the state or the county that you came from is paying for you to be there, regardless of where you committed the crime. Think about that for a minute. Why are you paying for a person that did a DUI that harmed no one to be locked up in Indiana, rather than the state the crime was committed in because that state didn't have enough room in its prison?

LEARN IT, BE IT, LEAD IT

As taxpayers, the American people need to ask themselves, "Where is every penny of my tax dollar being spent? Show me." You have the right to ask the government to prove it to you. They are not going to prove it to you, but you have the right to ask. Why aren't you questioning the $300 taken out of your paycheck every two weeks? The American people have no clue where their money actually goes or how it's distributed, or what becomes of a trillion-dollar spending plan signed by Congress. As the saying goes, "Why are you worried about money? They print more of it every day."

The rationale behind writing bad checks was this: Why should I be worried about a bank? They have plenty of money. At that time, a $25 fee was slapped on your account at 12:01 a.m. if your account was a penny short. How many fees do these people in this bank actually take from my

2,500 dollars that I got five years in prison for? Mind you, I might've only spent two years in jail, and the rest of that was spent on parole, but if I did anything, it was to prove that the banking system is just as broken as the prison system in this country, and people need to stop being willfully ignorant of these systems that can either put bread on the table, steal all your money, or punish you.

I'm not a criminal. I felt no remorse for defrauding the banks, and still believe I didn't deserve the sentence that was handed down to me, but everything took its natural course in the end, didn't it? I felt remorseful for having been caught, but I had no remorse or sympathy for the banks.

LEARN IT,
BE IT,
LEAD IT

They've got plenty of money to go around. This wasn't a person-to-person crime; in my mind, there was no victim. I was attacking an institution and rigged their pathetic systems to live out my wishes and dreams-the American Dream. Nobody died or was beset with violence. Yes, a crime was committed, but who have I hurt? A bank?!? Boo-hoo.

I was released from prison after serving two-and-a-half years on October 15, 1998. My parents picked me up from Pendleton, and we went home together. At the time I left prison, I weighed somewhere around 145 lbs. Technically, I was still in prison, just on parole during work release. I couldn't go back to McDonald's and work so I went to the Circle City Mall in Indianapolis, the one with the big round canopy that you drive up underneath. I did janitorial work at night when it was closed. I was the guy who wiped down the escalators and emptied the garbage and mopped the floors. You were paid minimum wage during work release, but you had to give the prison 50% of your wages because they are housing you. They are feeding you. So you don't get to cash your check. Your checks get signed off on before it goes into your account. Then 50% of that check is deducted for the state and 50% is put into your account.

Not long after that, I was driving my mom and dad to the airport, on their way to see my stepsister in Iowa. I was making my way through the terminal with them, and this guy came up to me and asked, "Are you a model?"

LEARN IT, BE IT, LEAD IT

"No," I replied, but I wasn't oblivious to the fact he was hitting on me. At this point, I'd never been into a gay bar. I didn't even know that one existed in Muncie-the Mark III Tap Room had been around since 1968, and it's the oldest LGBT bar in Indiana. I didn't know! No one talks about that shit, so I was in total ignorance of it! Our parents didn't want us to know it existed, but it's a hidden little gem of a gay bar in Muncie. I didn't even know what a twink was! I found out very, very quickly what a twink was, especially going to the Eagle, a gay leather bar, in Indianapolis.

Around this time, I met Jason at the Mark III Tap Room. Jason was the very first sexual experience that I had had outside of prison. He probably had a ten-inch, big, humongous pierced dick on him. He was a big boy, bear- type guy. It was a little scary at first because I wasn't used to such a bigger guy, and I was a lot skinnier. I enjoyed our short-lived relationship; it was nice. Don't get me wrong. It was nice to be with somebody just to be with them. We spent Christmas of '98 together, but I think it was moving too quickly for him. I'm a relationship hog, and while he had other friends. For me, it was different to be attached to somebody again. It only lasted for a hot month.

When I came out as being gay, Scottie married Tanya, who is African-American. They say that you don't instill ideals in your kids that you don't want them to reap or you don't want to reap in old age. I could never remember growing up with a Black person inside our

LEARN IT, BE IT, LEAD IT

home, not even for a visit. My father was a very racist man to the point when I came out, Scottie got married that same year to spite him. It killed my dad, and so he refused to have any contact with his grandkids. He refused to have any contact with me for being who I was. Even though he still loved me, it just wasn't his thing. When my mother, in her unconditional love, threatened to divorce him, he snapped out of it, and they're still together to this day.

Once work release and my probation ended, I worked temp jobs at the Maxon factory, where all day long we made parts for furnaces. It took a part out, put a part in, take a part out, put a part in. It wasn't me, but it was fun. My parents gave me their car, a Chevrolet Corsica, to get to and from work, and I put a rainbow Pride sticker on the back of it. Once I did that, the whole factory erupted. Not the kind of attention or environment I was looking for, nor what I expected, let's put it that way.

Being gay was a taboo subject, and simply not spoken of in our household while I was growing up. After prison, I started back on the ICOC path again. J.R.'s parents, John and Karen, picked me up from the outside dormitory, signed me out, and took me to ICOC once again. Being on work release, I had to be back by a certain time, but it didn't matter. I wanted to go back into that sense of belonging, that sense of church, that sense of everything. I had to confess all my sins to the discipler, and it finally came out. I was gay,

LEARN IT, BE IT, LEAD IT

J.R. was gay, and eventually, word got around to J.R.'s dad. Game over. Bye, ICOC.

J.R., meanwhile, had already moved on and lived in California, and he must've told his dad a long time before that. I wanted to shut the door forever in prison and start anew, change who I was and leave behind the Old Chris. Still, how could I play by ICOC rules and forget the emotional connection I felt with Eric in prison? That's who I am! I thought I could change all that by going back into the church, but it never happened. It never came to fruition.

About a year ago, I decided it was the right time to obtain a clean legal record, if not a spiritual one, and wash away all of my past troubles with the law. This would signal a turning point for me, and give me the courage and strength to tell my story. I spent the money to get a lawyer, John Quirk, and together we petitioned the prosecutor's office and the Nevada Highway Patrol to have my record completely expunged. Once they had completed their homework and made sure none of my prior convictions would give me trouble later, I'm happy to say that they wiped it all away like it never ever, ever happened.

In the state of Nevada, felons must register when they move there. No other state requires you to do that, and it's not like I committed a sexual crime-it was a white-collar crime-but I still had to register. It was ridiculous. Now even that crime is expunged from the registry and it's a little different for me. That's why I need to tell this story. If I don't

LEARN IT,
BE IT,
LEAD IT

tell you, it's like it never transpired. If I don't talk about the rape, it's like it never happened. If I don't talk about my life now that I'm retired, I'll never tell these stories, much less recall them. Why did I want all this off my record? I didn't want to be known as a felon for the rest of my life. Nobody wants that.

So I lived 24 years as a felon. In some way, this book you hold in your hands, all these stories about people and places, telling you about everything good and bad that has happened to me, is my way of letting it all go and closing this chapter of my life forever.

7

BEARS OF VEGAS

moved to Nevada in 2004, wanting a change. Starting over is never easy, but sometimes a change is necessary.

Why did I decide to move to Vegas? Back in Muncie, I was finally able to return to McDonald's and picked up some shifts at the 96th and Fisher location, but wasn't in any manager's position, although I stuck with that job until I moved. In addition, I also had some side hustles in real estate and as a CNA at Ball Memorial Hospital-anything I could do to get my life back on track.

That's when I met Ron; a short, stocky asshole who worked at a factory in Albany, Indiana, where he had previously served on the Albany Police Force for a time. Everybody knew Ron, and we had a great life together. We really did, and we even bought a home in Muncie. One day, my step-sister picked up the phone, called me, and said that she could no longer take care of my nephew, Alex. He was having problems in school and was taking enough Ritalin to knock down a horse.

LEARN IT, BE IT, LEAD IT

I decided that we should bring him to live with us, which he did for about two years. Ron and I drove to Belton, Missouri, to pick up Alex. The kid was a mess, honestly. We got him back home and the very first thing we did was take him to see a doctor. My pediatrician was still practicing so that's where we took him, and he gave me a dose of reality.

"This is not what you need, Chris," He said. "This is not what this kid needs. He needs discipline."

I'm a humongous disciplinarian, thanks to my father's unyielding sense of it. I was raised to be polite and always say, "Yes, sir. No, sir. Yes, ma'am," and that's what I expected out of Alex. Meanwhile, I was working at a Rent-A-Center and was doing about an hour commute into Indianapolis and then an hour back to Muncie. That's two hours on top of a nine- to ten-hour shift.

While I was unaware of it at the time it occurred, while I was juggling these various jobs, Ron molested my nephew as well as another young gentleman, a half-cousin. My step-sister immediately scooped Alex back up and left with him. Ron was arrested at work, went to jail, and within about three or four days was dismissed and no charges were ever filed against him.

My discipline worked well, and by the time Alex left us, he was very popular in school and a straight-A student. He'd been weaned off the medication and was overall much better off. So when these allegations came out against Ron, I honestly did not believe them, but it didn't matter. I had a

LEARN IT,
BE IT,
LEAD IT

duty and responsibility towards Alex, because number one, he's family, and two, he's living in my home, and three, why didn't I know? It didn't make sense. I still haven't talked to Alex to this day.

I was completely oblivious to the whole horrific incident, and all the sordid details. How often and when this had occurred were kept from me by our family attorney, who explained that the less I knew about the situation, the better, but I couldn't repair the damage that had already been done on multiple fronts. I left Ron and moved back in with mom and dad until Vegas beckoned. It's the relationships that you build up in these very small towns, that you nurture and keep, that turnaround and bite you in the ass. In the face of adversity, it was time for a change for the better. Midwest guys, they move. That's what made me move to Las Vegas.

I'd been to Vegas once before, and on a separate occasion, I went to the International Bear Rendezvous in San Francisco. At the time, I didn't even know what a "bear" was. I had no idea that there were different segmented groups within the gay community including twinkies, bears, cubs, all that shit. I went to IBR because I wanted a sexual experience even though I was still with Ron. I just wanted to have fucking fun, right? And I wanted to go somewhere I had never been, which was San Francisco. The bear culture to me has never been big until these past couple of years with Mike since we've reached middle age and are fatter. It's a bear thing.

LEARN IT, BE IT, LEAD IT

The first time I went to IBR, I was 180 lbs. with a size 34-36 waist, and I looked really good! I had all these bears coming in and out of my hotel room like revolving doors. One guy specifically was from Montana, a hefty, bigger guy. I thought I was in love, but I was still just a kid by bear standards. I wasn't in love. I was in lust. While there, I met a couple, Steve and Mike (different Mike) who have remained my friends ever since I arrived in Sin City. I stayed with them for about a week when I got to Vegas, even had a three-way with them, but I didn't really hang out with them.

Instead, I was hanging out at the Buffalo, a now-defunct gay bar. There, I met James, who I thought was going to be the love of my life-6'3", tattooed, little dick, but a humongous bottom. We spent one hell of a night together but I didn't have a fucking clue what I was doing. I moved in with James, and it was probably one of the best decisions I made at the time because I knew I'd finally arrived. I'm a Midwest boy so I understood all the risks I was taking in the name of fun, bodily fluids, and armpits-bear stuff. Above all, I'd felt emancipated from Indiana. The best of times is *now*.

I will say that as a gay man, I felt more protected by my support system in Muncie than in Vegas. Even though I'm a minority here and I have always been a minority as a gay male, employers can sometimes fire you because you're gay. Being fired for being gay wasn't my biggest fear. My biggest fear was my past catching up to me and some of my offenses appearing in background checks. Nevada has a seven-year policy, so they can only go back seven years in the records to see what you've done if anything. When I got here, I had to get a recommendation from Mc McCopCo in Indianapolis in order to work at McDonald's inside Circus Circus, which was a very big deal, and I absolutely loved it. At this point, James and I were playing the whole married couple game, and I lived with him for two months before his lease was up, then we rented a house together.

While I was having the time of my life working under the Big Top for McDonald's inside Circus Circus, James and I decided to break it off. Following James, there was Travis, who only lasted about two months. Travis was very much into "hippie stuff "-auras, everything has an energy, he could see "grids," whatever the hell they are-but really he was a big ol' bottom. I felt like the biggest top in all of God's creation!

From Travis, I moved on to Logan, who I met at Backstreets, which is now Charlie's. Logan and I were together for almost two years. Mike and I have been together since 2006, so Logan and I must have gotten together in the early part of 2005. It wasn't meant to be. One day, Logan got a new credit card in the mail, and he asked me to take the card, go down the street, and fill up the car with gas; a simple request I didn't think anything of.

On the way there, I stopped at a grocery store and bought a few groceries with the card. Not long after, Logan got the

statement in the mail saw the charges and went bonkers and ballistic. We broke up. It was over, and I moved out of the house, away from Logan, and into another house off the street by the name of Shinnecock Hills Avenue, but most everyone calls it Shiny Cock. This was the house I lived in when I first met Mike, but I hadn't heard the last of Logan by a long shot.

After almost fifteen years of working on and for McDonald's, I decided to work for Wendy's, which paid more. This is where I met Brian, a manager who absolutely hated me, so much so that I called him the Wolf of Las Vegas. Despite his assholisms or because of them, I thought I deserved a break and decided to cash in on a vacation to Hawaii that Ron and I had won during a charitable AIDS event, and it was still within the two-year deadline to take the trip.

I decided to take a good friend along with me, Michael, who I'd been friends with for years, and while I was on vacation, the Wolf of Las Vegas decided to do an audit of the food inventory at the restaurant. It turns out I was missing a few bags of chicken breasts, of all things. I was on the beach in Hawaii when the Wolf called.

"Chris, do you know where I'm standing?" The cards had been dealt.

"You're probably in my store because you're an asshole so that means that you're doing an audit, right?" It's as if I can see his hand already.

LEARN IT,
BE IT,
LEAD IT

"Yeah, we're doing an audit," he replied, but I had a vacation on the brain and could care less. "Can you tell me where four cases of chicken breasts are? It says they were transferred."

"Did my assistant transfer them out? I don't know. Dude, I'm on vacation."

"No." And here the Wolf lays down a decisive card: "I think you stole them."

"I stole four cases of breasts?!?" I called his bluff.

"No, but you're trying awfully hard to make your food costs look better." He thinks he's won. He has no idea.

"Brother," and here I play the ace up my sleeve. "You know what? I fucking hate you. I fucking quit." I quit that night while I was on vacation, and while I didn't have much money on hand, I felt confident I could easily land another job when I returned from my trip. James met me at the airport, picked me up, and took me back to Shiny Cock, and I barely got comfortable in my home when there was a knock on my door.

"Christopher Byrd?" It was the Las Vegas police. "Yes, sir. That's me."

"We have a warrant for your arrest," the police said. "For what? I didn't do anything." Turns out, Logan called the police and claimed I had used his credit card illegally to obtain the gas and the groceries, but I forgot to tell the cops one important fact- we lived together. Logan wanted me arrested at the airport because he was the one who I

LEARN IT, BE IT, LEAD IT

was supposed to take to Hawaii, not Michael, that spiteful bitch. Back to jail, I went, and I stayed there for about five hours before I was released. There were no charges, no warrant, no bail, I was just let go. A week or so later, I get a call from a detective who informs me that all charges have been dropped for obvious reasons.

I needed a release after all of Logan's bullshit, and one evening I went to the Eagle with my best friend Lars, who has since passed away, and his husband Mike, and they introduced me to the man who will rearrange my entire world for the better-my future husband, Mike. Oddly enough, we had met two years previous. Funny how the cosmos puts people in your life, literally sets them right in front of you, then bashes you over the head to make you realize this is the one who'll stick around this time!

When I first met Mike, I was with Logan. He was jealous and hated that fact. Logan was not a bear. Logan was skinnier; more twinkish, but not exactly a cub. He has a nice husband now and they live in San Diego. We say "Hi" to each other on Facebook and that's about it. To this day, I absolutely hate him for the stolen credit card stunt he pulled on me.

As you've no doubt gathered by now, I've always been opportunistic and ready to embrace the right situation to better myself and make some money if at all possible, but this time it was going to be through hard work. I wanted to be my own boss.

LEARN IT,
BE IT,
LEAD IT

In 2007, I decided to open a chain of cell phone stores, Byrd Phones, and we did a pretty brisk business for a couple of years. I really enjoyed coming up with clever marketing schemes and advertisements to drive business and get customers into our four locations-three in Vegas and another back home in Muncie. In a particularly well-known ad, I actually used this baby picture of me from when I was about two years old with this 70's blond bob hairstyle. I had blonde hair back then and now I have brown hair, although it's thinning on top.

In the picture, I'm holding a phone up to my ear, but the phone is turned upside down with the speaker in my mouth, and I'm flipping the bird to the camera. It actually became a very famous picture around Muncie after it was published in a local magazine. Later, I used this same picture in an advertisement campaign in Vegas Magazine. Since I was flipping the bird to the camera, it just made sense to feature me in the ad with the slogan "Be the Byrd," and that became the marketing gimmick for the stores.

I do want to give a special shout-out to one of my best employees and closest friends who worked with me side- by side in the stores-Julie, the "Blonde Barbie." I truly cherish and love her; she was not only the face of the store but also the brand. We had a lot in common. Julie was once a highly successful Escrow agent who worked for Washington Mutual, then moved to Vegas and completely reinvented herself. I wouldn't have been nearly as successful if not for

LEARN IT, BE IT, LEAD IT

her dedication, loyalty, and friendship in those days. In fact, Mike says that he always knows when I've spoken to Julie on the phone because my whole attitude improves.

Another side-hustle I've recently taken up in the past year is massage. I love to do massages. I'm a natural-born top, so you know I love that sense of contact and intensity when it comes to rubbing on soft and supple to ripped, rock-hard bodies. Being a proud bear, of course, I had to name the company Bears sage.

In that spirit, I've also created a new Facebook group called Bears of Vegas. We're close to 400 members now. When I was starting up Bears sage, I advertised on another Facebook group, our bitter rival, Bears of *Las* Vegas. Their admins decided I was posting too much, so I decided to create my own group. There's a pretty diverse bear scene in Vegas and not everyone gets equal representation. People are tired of cliques anyway; it's such a gay thing. We need to be more open and inclusive as a community, more forgiving, and less judgmental.

The bears of Vegas have been both accepting and kind of assholes at the same time. They welcomed me in the best possible way, made me feel comfortable with my sexuality, and w e r e thankful for a newfound place to call home. Whether I was loved or not by some of the men in my life, at least I wasn't in Indiana. I'd made a name for myself in Vegas in the early 2000s, far away from my hometown, where the ghosts of so many bad memories still haunt those all-

LEARN IT, BE IT, LEAD IT

too-familiar streets of Muncie. Everything had changed for me, not without some bumps in the road, but ultimately for the better.

8

MIKE

ike and I were destined to be together. Even before we were married, whether we knew we were meant to be together at the time or not, it seemed to be written in the stars. We've been together 16 years, which is forever in gay years, similar to dog years. In gay years, the time Mike and I have really spent together seems almost like double time.

For Mike and myself, longevity and commitment are the common bonds. Mike is my best friend. Mike is a person that I align with and is one of the sweetest individuals I've ever met, with the biggest heart. We live in Vegas with our dog, Scamper. We own eight properties, and we're financially comfortable enough that we could up and leave Vegas and still collect rent on the houses we own together.

While I first met Mike in person in 2006, he was a professional bodybuilder and worked at the MGM Grand Casino. We'd actually spoken online two years prior when we connected over the gay dating site Men4Men.com, back

LEARN IT, BE
IT, LEAD IT

when you had to suffer through that ear-splitting dial-up tone to connect to the internet. We must've sensed something special because I do remember talking to him over the phone at that time, but nothing really came of that initial meeting online. At first, we sent messages back and forth to each other, but then he gave me his number. We didn't even realize we'd connected before until we were discussing it after we had already been together for a couple of years. I guess that just goes to show you how small of a village Vegas really is!

Remember when Paris Hilton was saying her trademark

line, "That's hot?" That was my big saying when I first met Mike, this hometown Las Vegas native, who at first thought I was an egotistical prick when we met in person. I met him at the Eagle; he was wearing a pair of Daisy Dukes, a cut-off shirt, crew socks, and a pair of work boots-a bear by definition. He looked like a Tom of Finland illustration. That night was memorable, not just because of Mike, but also because there was a dude with a funnel in his mouth sitting in the bathroom, and he was the urinal.

We were introduced to each other by Larzs, who I mentioned has since passed. Lars probably wouldn't even recognize the Eagle now if he was still alive, ever since they painted the whole damn place pink and turned it into a drag bar. Back then, the Eagle was known for its bears and you could either be naked, in a jockstrap, or underwear, but if you were naked, you got your drinks for free-well drinks,

LEARN IT, BE IT, LEAD IT

but free. During that time, the Eagle had a dark hallway with holes through the wall, a big cross on the back wall next to the pool table, and two bars on either side of the room.

I was standing up against the back wall like I usually did, minding my own business. I'd just gotten back from Hawaii, fed up with the Wolf's and Logan's antics, and ready to give up and move back to Indiana. I had enough of Vegas! I wanted to move back home. Fuck it! I can make my parents happy. Here I come, Mom! Little did I know, that attitude was about to change drastically.

I was standing against the wall, wearing a small shirt, little bay shorts, and a pair of flip flops with my foot against the wall. Lars came from across the room, and said, "I got someone for you to meet. Come and meet him!" I tried brushing him off; I wasn't in the mood to meet anyone new, but he didn't back down. I just had to meet this guy, said Lars, before I went back home to Indiana.

And so, I met Mike. Michael, Larzs's husband, went and grabbed Mike and told him the same thing he had to meet me. At first glance, I didn't think anything of it. In fact, I was thinking that I'd play hard to get. After that, we all went to this little cafe off Tropicana across from the Eagle that stays open all night. There must've been about eight of us there because this other group of guys joined us. We stayed there talking, getting to know each other 'til about four in the morning, then I got up to leave. Before I did, I told Mike

LEARN IT, BE IT, LEAD IT

that I was going to Hawks, a bathhouse. No big deal here's my number, call me in the morning, Stud.

This motherfucker followed me to Hawks, where, you guessed it, we had some pretty nasty sex that night. Afterward, I got his phone number. It was right around his birthday on September 1st. I had just turned 30. Mike was turning 40. Later, I called and told him I got him a birthday present: We're going to take a road trip. He didn't know me from anybody, but he actually got into the car with me and we drove to the Grand Canyon. He had never visited there, and that was his birthday present. However, wisely, he told a few people where he was going, my phone number, and my license plate number in case he didn't show back up.

During the three or four-hour drive to the Grand Canyon,

we had long conversations about life and love and really got to know each other. We were either destined to be together or we were going to kill each other in two days on this road trip, but I really got to know him as an individual, and after that, there was no separating us.

Mike is different from all these other guys. I have the Midwest look. I have Midwest cooking skills. I am the very definition of Midwest. It's a whole way of life. City guys like Mike, who grew up in Las Vegas, have no idea. We are into the television show *Yellowstone*. We watch it a lot, but he knows nothing about riding a horse or mucking (cleaning) a stall out. Growing up in the Midwest, who hasn't done that? Everyone in my family had at one point or another. You

LEARN IT, BE IT, LEAD IT

might not remember it, but I guarantee anyone from the Midwest has mucked a stall at one point. I guess opposites, like the country mouse and the city mouse, do attract!

On December 19, 2006, Mike proposed to me. We were at 11 Fornaio inside the New York, New York casino. I have the menu from that night hanging on my wall at home. I had just closed up McDonald's at Circus Circus and he wanted to go out to dinner. After my shift, I was about ready to pass out and fall asleep, but off we went to see Zumanity, and afterward, we went out for dinner

I'm very Midwestern-I like plain cheesecake. That's my dessert; I don't even look at the dessert menu. I was halfway through dinner, ready to clock out, and Mike took my phone away from me because people were calling me from work, and he wanted my full attention.

"We're just going to eat dinner, okay?" He said, and a waitress approached our table.

"Would you like to see a dessert menu?" She asked. No, I just want cheesecake. I'm good.

"Sir, I really think you need to see this dessert menu," She insisted. No, I just-"Here, I'm going to bring you a dessert menu."

Now I was getting really pissy because I just wanted cheesecake!

"You really need to look at that menu, sir." She handed me the menu. Mike had set up all this in advance by himself.

LEARN IT, BE
IT, LEAD IT

The menu contained a poem he composed himself-not cheesecake. The poem read:

Christopher -

I've waited so long
through the good
Through the strife
to have someone in
my life Someone so
special a man so
sweet

Tonight the desert
menu cannot be
complete Before
you I was empty
never complete
Menus have
choices like so
many I've made
A taste a sample
but they all seem
to fade Tonight I
realize this love
that we've made
Not just a taste so
much more than
a treat

I see now why you and
I were destined to meet
So how do I say the
words that I feel how I
do Each its own reason
my love grows for you

So nervous so happy I don't think I
can wait

Be it stars, prayers, or fate I
loved our first date Somehow
that day I knew this would be

I don't know if I saved you, I know you saved me "Broken Roads" or "A Reckless Soul"

I know now
alone I can no
longer go
Down here I
am

Yes on bended knee

So now I ask... Will You Marry Me?

Mike and I were married inside the chapel at Planet Hollywood on 07/07/07; July 7th, 2007. To this day, the license plate on my truck is 777LDS-or "777 Last Day

LEARN IT,
BE IT,
LEAD IT

Single." At that time, gay marriage wasn't legal in Nevada, so we got a domestic partnership, which was just barely legal in Nevada. Mike had never been married before, and as for me, well, you know the rest...

Our domestic partnership is #252 in the state of Nevada. We were some of the first 500 people to be issued a domestic partnership license before marriage was legal. Two years after that, in 2009, we went to California and we made it legal after the Supreme Court made gay marriage the law of the land.

While we had discussed marriage before, it was always

a big deal as to who was going to propose first, although my expectations were such that I thought Mike would end up proposing to me. I worked too much and too hard, so I really didn't care. We were either going to be together or we are not going to be together, but he actually got down on one knee and proposed.

After the wedding, we spent our honeymoon in Muncie, and Mike met the family. I was scared at first, but I wanted my family to celebrate our union and was pleasantly surprised that Mike got along really well with my family, including my father, and he was treated like a fourth Byrd son in many ways. We love my folks, and especially Mike- for him it's like having another set of parents. Again, we have a great relationship with them now. We'd soon learn that any time spent with our parents is quality time- precious, limited time.

LEARN IT, BE IT, LEAD IT

Mike makes me laugh. He is a funny, witty individual, kind of like a dog in a way. He is very loyal. Throw whatever you like at him, beat him with a newspaper, and he would still be licking your nose. He is an extremely loyal individual. He's my best friend. We do everything together. We don't really have friends like other couples do. We stay to ourselves. We go to the movies. We come home. We go to work. We come home. These days, we don't work at all, which I'll discuss more in the next chapter.

It's kind of hard to put Mike into words. We've only had three big fights than I can count and that's it. It has evolved into a forever relationship. Well, in about 2015, I thought about leaving Mike. We were in that seven-year itch rough patch bullshit stage that every couple goes through. Somebody had shown interest in me and Mike always said, "Leave then, damn it! Leave!" I think he was hurt more than anything because I gave this individual my personal time. So that's another reason we don't really have close friends outside of our relationship. Mike knows that I do my thing and I know Mike does his thing, and it's never discussed. It's best that way and works for us.

I remember we were sitting at his house during our first Christmas together in 2006. We were talking, going over our pasts and stuff like that, and it took me almost a whole year to tell Mike about mine because I was scared. People don't react very well when you tell them you've been to prison, or what happened that you ended up there. Both his parents

LEARN IT,
BE IT,
LEAD IT

passed without ever knowing my true past, which is kind of scary and sad to think about.

Both Mike and I love our parents dearly, and one of the biggest tests our relationship faced was when his mother, Judith, passed away on December 12, 2012. If the course of our relationship was divided into eras, this would be a big one for us. Twelve always seems to be a meaningful recurring number when it comes to significant events in our relationship, and it was a turning point in Mike's life.

Since they lived in Vegas, his mom and his dad, Ron, became very much a part of our lives. For me, I gained a second family. In 2011, not long before the operation that would lead to a series of health setbacks for Judy, they celebrated their 50th wedding anniversary, and we had a humongous party for them at Maggiano's. I grew very close to Judy and felt I could actually talk to his mom more than I think Mike even talked to his mom. My parents are very wonderful people, but they didn't know how to accept me. Ron and Judy just wanted their son to be happy, so it was a different type of acceptance and they were very easy to bond with. I managed their properties, and we loved going out to dinner with them. Since Mike is an only child, I was accepted as a second son.

That same Thanksgiving, we invited them and dozens of other people to our home. Judith loved my mom and liked being around her family, and Judy's sister Sherry and her husband Randy had flown in from Washington to see her

LEARN IT, BE IT, LEAD IT

and attend the SEMA Car Show. Everybody was at the house and they were having a blast. In fact, I still have a photo of Judy and Sherry from the Thanksgiving dinner that year.

About a year or so afterward, Judy went in for surgery to fix a blood clot in her abdomen after doctors had already taken care of a clot in her leg three months prior, but something felt off and Judy wasn't having it. Mike tried to reassure her, but she dreaded the surgery and felt something bad was going to happen this time around.

I think Madea said it best: "Between the age of 40 and 50, it's called the roadblock of life." For me, it's been a roadblock where everybody hates everybody, everybody is disgruntled with everything, and you can become a very bitter individual yourself if you don't keep things in perspective. Mike's parents were getting sick and dying. My parents were getting sick; their health has gotten better. I can never tell Mike "I know how you feel" when it comes to Judy because my mom is still alive. I think if I ever lost my mom, I would go crazy. He is handling it better than I have, but he has had a little bit of time to deal with it since. Unfortunately, after the surgery, the doctor had Judy's kidneys offline for too long and while he tried to save her, he just couldn't do it. She was on life support for about three weeks in ICU. Mike, Ron, and I were called in to make a decision.

Judith was an angel, then and now. She sits in an urn in the dining room alongside Ron, who passed away this last year. It was a hard time for everyone.

9

2021

This past year, 2021, has been our season in hell. If the hard times prove anything, it's always best to circle the wagons and hang on tight, because it's about to

get a helluva lot worse. I had to get this all down, and this is another reason why this story contained in this book even exists.

After Judy passed, we all went on a cruise, one of our favorite pre-COVID vacations to take, and we brought along Ron's side of the family-Mike's aunts, uncles, all their kids, everyone on this big family cruise that left from Seattle. Mike and I shared a cabin with Ron, and he wanted to be a Boy Scout, so he took the top bunk. We slept below him. It was pretty funny, actually. Mike and I were like, "Oh great! Cruise vacation and your dad is sleeping above us!"

We knew that Ron was having problems with his motor skills, but we didn't know to what extent or the cause. We soon found out. He got up one night to use the bathroom, missed the ladder, fell out of his bunk, hit his head on the

LEARN IT, BE IT, LEAD IT

mirror, and rolled onto the floor. He had stitches put in his head by the doctor on the cruise ship, who also took some x-rays to make sure he was okay.

Back in Vegas, once the stitches were removed, the doctors did a CAT scan and found out that Ron had early- onset Alzheimer's and white matter disease. We really didn't know how to accept this difficult news. Things were never quite the same for Ron after Judy had passed. His personality had completely changed. Dad was extremely scared to stay at his home by himself, a home that Mike and I had built for him in 2019.

About this time, Ron met a woman named Joan. Mike hated this woman instantly, and she even did a background check on Ron and knew what he owned within a month and a half of the start of their relationship. Mind you, Ron and Judy were high school sweethearts, so he didn't know any better than to be in a relationship with someone. Mike immediately put all of dad's assets into a trust.

Joan wanted to live with Ron but didn't want to live in the home that Ron and Judy built and had lived in together, so they started looking at new homes. We had a home built for both of them and Ron took out a loan on the home but left Joan off of the paperwork. Once she found that out, she left Ron, which left Mike and I with Ron and his advancing case of Alzheimer's. To better care for Ron, we made a room in our home just for him.

LEARN IT, BE IT, LEAD IT

Every Tuesday was family night. No matter what we did, we put our life on hold, because that was Ron's night. He came to the house then, or any other night he wanted to come over. On Tuesday nights we made dinner, and then every other weekend or so we would do movie nights, just to keep Ron active and moving.

Things got worse for Ron mentally, and we couldn't help what was going on inside his head. Once, when he came to visit, it got so bad that Ron thought there were ghosts in the house and he said he could hear voices of people who weren't there. At one point, he went out and chopped all the hedges down in front of the house because he thought people were looking through them at us sitting inside. We had to put motion sensor lights all around the house, and it would light up just like a prison if you moved around outside, but Ron's safety was more important.

Once Ron and Joan called it quits, Ron was off his rocker and his mental and physical health continued to slide downhill. Without Judy, life seemed to gradually slip through his fingers. We were afraid to lose him, but how was I to know I would nearly lose Mike, too?

On January 7, 2021, Mike went into the hospital with COVID-19, and within a week, he was admitted into the ICU and fell into a coma for a month. He had a stroke. At the same time, Ron went to the hospital. As the medics were putting Ron into the ambulance on the stretcher, he said, "I just want you to know I love you. I just want out of jail." Maybe the jail was his mind, finally trying to free himself from the brain that had betrayed his health. How do you deal with hearing that somebody just wants out of the jail in their own mind?

Mike is an only child. Judy, his mom, who was an angel on this earth, had passed. With Mike in the hospital, according to Ron's will, the duties fell to me to make important decisions about his health. Ron was 79 years old when Alzheimer's took his life, but before that, I had to make the hardest decision I was yet to make for a beloved parent, and I made the decision to put Ron into hospice care.

I never thought I would have to make that type of decision. That particular day, on a whim, I was in Primm, Nevada, home to the largest gas station on that stretch of 1-15 on the border of California and Nevada, so I could enjoy a White Castle burger-one of the few places in our neck of the woods you can get a White Castle burger. I didn't have much else to do that day, but within twenty minutes of the doctor calling me about putting Ron in hospice, I got the phone call about Mike.

I was sitting in the truck, bawling like a baby at one of the gas pumps, on the phone having an emotional conversation about Ron's condition with his sisters, Mike's aunts. Of course, they were not happy with the decision to put Ron in hospice, or the fact that I told the doctors to add a feeding tube since he wasn't eating in the hospital. Within about twenty minutes, the hospital calls and wants to know if it's

LEARN IT,
BE IT,
LEAD IT

okay to intubate Mike since he was having trouble breathing. I told the doctor to do everything they could to save him, and they assured me they would, including putting Mike on life support, but only as a last resort.

Mike and I have advance directives about our health care, and I hope to God I never have to make this kind of decision again, but when all else fails, it's okay to resort to a higher power. I had to talk to Judy. I came home and she was sitting on the shelf in her urn in the dining room. I will never forget this. I went down on my knees. I prayed. I talked to Judy and asked for a trade-off; she could have Ron but she couldn't take Mike. Not yet. I think it was one of the hardest conversations I've ever had in my entire life.

How would I cope knowing that I was going to lose someone who loved and accepted me like his own son, or face losing my husband and being forced to continue on without him when we'd worked so hard for what we had together? Ultimately, the trade-off was that God let me keep Mike, but he wouldn't be the same Mike as he was before COVID-19.

On February 19th, Ron passed without knowing the real Chris. He was one of the most honest men that I have ever met and he died not knowing the real me. I'd been married to his son for all of sixteen years by this point, and he never knew that I had been in prison. His last words to me were, "Tell Mike I love him." I don't know if my dad would say the same thing to me on his deathbed.

LEARN IT, BE IT, LEAD IT

With Ron gone, having to decide what to do with Mike fell squarely on me. When Mike came back from the hospital, he had lost 70 pounds and had to relearn how to walk and how to use the bathroom, amongst other everyday tasks people take for granted. I couldn't give up on him, no matter what. You build love together and you really don't know how to let your best friend go. I couldn't let Mike go. I know it sounds very selfish, but I really wouldn't know what to do with myself. I couldn't tell Mike for a month that his father had passed because I was told not to by the doctor, who said his condition could regress and he'd end up back in the hospital.

If Mike was gone, I wouldn't have a clue. I've always taken care of Mike. In relationships, being the one that takes care of the other person and knowing that, if necessary, you'll have to humble yourself enough to wipe your loved one's ass if you have to, it's not always easy, but you just do it because you love that individual. I think that's where a lot of people don't understand how two guys could actually love each other. That's how important Mike is to me. After all this crap that happened, it shed a lot of light on how strong and resilient our relationship was. Amazing what you learn about each other when your loved ones are on life support!

Thankfully, beyond all possible outcomes, Mike's home now. He has lingering COVID-19 effects. For example, he coughs a lot. The way I was raised, you don't cough or sneeze in public. Now when Mike coughs in public, I look

LEARN IT,
BE IT,
LEAD IT

at him and tell him to shut up. He also has some memory issues, and can't always recall anything that happened a day or two ago, and most of the time his mind just kind of goes to left field. I may have gotten the trade-off I prayed to God and Judy for after all, because in some ways, I got to keep Ron a little bit since Mike is becoming his dad.

Still, I couldn't do the rental homes by myself, nor the finances, and even then there's plenty of stuff I couldn't do by myself that Mike did for our businesses in addition to Ron's and Judy's businesses after we inherited all their homes and assets. But there's no replacing Mike or his parents, ever.

I would rather be working today than retired, after working in even know he was an only child!

About ten years ago, I was running an apartment complex called Ruby Harbor on the corner of Sahara and Nellis, and I was the Junior Regional Manager at the time of four housing communities. On the opposite side of a 6-foot common wall was its sister community, Verdant Fields. In

LEARN IT, BE IT, LEAD IT

one year, Verdant Fields had a total of six murders on the property, while my property stayed secure and thriving.

I used to say you couldn't pay me $10 million a year to run Verdant Fields. But after working for the rental company for almost four of the past ten years, even though they owned two of the biggest and also two of the worst communities in Vegas, I guess you could say I'd had enough. I was passed up for a promotion and that's what made me consider resigning, as well as the incident I'm about to describe to you. I had worked in the Junior Regional Manager's position for years and was told I would not be a good fit for the Regional Manager's position. No worries, so here's my two- week notice. My boss' boss hated me because I was gay. In fact, in my two-week notice, I called him a knuckle-dragging, cave-dwelling, KKK fraternity brother member. I didn't just burn that bridge, I blew it up, but it needed to be said. Both Ruby Harbor and Verdant Fields went downhill after I left and soon resembled trailer parks.

But just when I thought I was out, they pulled me back in. Even though I interviewed for the new position and was turned down, I wasn't told that I'd be managing a new property in the meantime two days after I had turned in the notice. Much to my surprise, I was assigned to manage Verdant Fields. I hyped myself up, told myself that I could make this work, and so from April to September of 2021, I did just that-but the end was coming sooner than I thought.

LEARN IT, BE IT, LEAD IT

One day, a young lady walked into my office along with her mother. She was on housing assistance, and later we found out that there were eight other individuals living inside that apartment. She came into my office, cussing and screaming up a storm. I sat there dumbfounded and offered to hit the reset button on the whole conversation. Her mom even grabs her shoulder and tries to reason with her.

"Hey, honey, he is trying to help you."

"Shut the fuck up!" Her daughter roared back at her.

Now, if it were me, coming from where I came from, I would be sent flying through three walls, busted a couple of front teeth, and wounded with an eyeball dangling out of my skull for saying that to my mother. This kid was probably in her twenties and the mom couldn't have been much more than fifteen years her elder, and after she screamed at her, her mom just looked down at the floor like nothing had happened.

The situation escalated. I stood up behind my desk, and my assistant Loni, who was at least 74 years old, ran into my office, telling the girl, "Honey, it's time for you to go." Then the girl started cussing and screaming at Loni!

"Shut the fuck up, you old bitch!"

That was the moment. I was done. I left the office, and everyone could see me turning every shade of red that you could possibly imagine. That night I came home and I told Mike what happened at the office.

LEARN IT, BE IT, LEAD IT

"Honey, why don't you just quit? Just retire?" It was September 13, 2021. I took Mike's advice, and that was the end of it. That was the end of my property management career aside from the homes we own now.

I was the guy that you came to if you took over a community that was in dire straits. It may have been the shittiest property known to man, falling apart, riddled with drugs and gang activity, but you wanted to make a name for it. In the past, other apartment complexes I've managed were four-star rated communities by the time I was finished with them. Even Verdant Fields, when I left it, was being improved upon and we were at 98% occupancy. We were hitting delinquency goals even in the middle of COVID-19, where no one paid. I still got payments. You name it, we were doing it. But that sad, misguided young lady who stormed into my office was my breaking point. To stand there and cuss your mom out? No thanks. I didn't need to work.

I had won awards as a property manager and turned dumps into habitable, safe communities. Why didn't I get promoted? Because I was gay. Sometimes the grass isn't always greener on the other side of the fence. This was the point in time where I needed to learn that lesson. God really opened my eyes up because I told Him I would never go and run Verdant Fields, but He must've had a sick sense of humor, and decided to play one last evil joke on me.

I tell everybody this: Make your money work for you. Don't work for your money. I was working too hard in

LEARN IT,
BE IT,
LEAD IT

the property management business to be treated like that. When I married Mike, I had no idea how much in assets and property he and his family had, and while it's still not my money, I married into it all the same. At the end of 2021, we closed on our 8th rental home here in Las Vegas.

Both Mike and I had to go through a lot to get what we have. We thought we were going to have to fight his relatives over Ron's and Judy's assets, but thankfully Mike put it all in a trust. If you own one home, go out and get a trust tomorrow. It's the best advice I can give anybody. It protects your assets and creates an LLC. The state has absolutely no right to it, and your money is working for you at that point, rather than you working for it. It's a business account, it's accruing interest, any paychecks are deposited into it and that's when you're actually paying yourself.

Many individuals have no idea that the real key to my success in property management or any business venture is to simply listen. Judge Judy once said, "God gave you two ears and one mouth. Learn to use your ears and not your mouth." If people just shut up and listen, it's amazing what you can learn, and that's what I mean by learning it, be it, and lead it.

Whether you're a fly on the wall or a piece of shit on someone's shoe, you can put on a suit tomorrow, go into a meeting, and come out with more knowledge-just like a felon can while in prison. Put on an orange jumpsuit, go to

LEARN IT, BE IT, LEAD IT

jail, and come out with more knowledge than you had when you went in. You are a product of your surroundings.

Learn it, be it, lead it. Thanks for listening.

EPILOGUE

I want to thank some very important people in my life, including my parents, Mary and Ken Byrd, my ex-wife

Mandy, my beautiful husband Mike, my brothers Scottie and Jerred, and my late father-in-law, Ron, Mike's father, who treated me like his own son. Without their love, support,

and unwavering ability to teach me the hard lessons, I simply wouldn't be alive to tell this story today.

Mike and I have been together for sixteen years and his family was the most accepting family in the world. Reading this book might be a little bit of a jolt for some of my family members, and that's OK. Mike and I have a very long journey ahead of us. When I try to envision Mike and his needs in the next ten years, I'm probably going to have to bring in some help at some point, because Mike is going to get worse. It's very likely his memory, cognitive, and motor abilities will continue to deteriorate as the sun goes down. At least I'll be there to share it with him.

There's still a lot I need to learn, a lot of living left to do, but it has to happen before I can lead it. I want to keep my businesses growing, too. My advice to anyone is to buy dirt. If you buy dirt, make a plan and build a home on it. Do so, because everybody needs someplace to live with a roof over

their head. As a manager of rental properties, I have a slogan that gives our tenants peace of mind and assures them that we know what we're doing, that we're different from any other landlord they've dealt with, and that slogan is:

"Improving and empowering the way you live and doing business with love and compassion."

I truly believe in this, and it's even on the side of my truck. Ron created his rental property business in 1987 and focused on affordable housing for individuals, and it's in that same spirit I do business with our tenants. Show them love, and they'll love their homes, and your properties, in return.

This book, in that sense, is a work of love. There are so many more chapters, so many more stories that this book could contain, but now's the time for me to lead others who may be struggling and going through rough patches in their own life, and hopefully, those people will find love in between the words on these pages and begin to see their own lives in a different, brighter, more radiant light.

Don't write your story down on the pages of your life without knowing who you are. Let others know who you are, and be honest and truthful in that! Let go of pain and hurt. At the end of the day, you must become your own biggest fan, and fuck those who refuse to believe in you or have doubts about who you are.

Believe in yourself.